MW01229806

Kids Across Kulture Book 2

"Bracey Beeks Discovers the UK Wonders"

By

Peter Clarke

Table of Contents

Chapter 1: Introduction

Bracey Beeks, the young adventurer with a heart full of curiosity and a thirst for knowledge, was about to embark on a brand-new journey. This time, his quest led him to the enchanting world of British culture.

Welcome to a World of Diversity and Friendship

The air was tinged with excitement as Bracey set foot on the vibrant and historic lands of the United Kingdom. A world of diversity and friendship awaited him, and he was ready to embrace the enchanting tapestry of British culture.

The United Kingdom was a place where ancient castles stood alongside modern cities, where rich traditions were woven into daily life, and where the people were known for their warmth and hospitality.

As Bracey took his first steps on this adventure, he felt a sense of wonder and awe. He knew that this journey would unravel stories of history, tales of friendship, and the magic that made the UK a unique part of the world.

With each chapter, Bracey would explore the different aspects of British culture. From the delicious cuisine to the lively festivals, the iconic landmarks to the charming countryside, he was about to uncover the rich tapestry that made the UK so special.

And so, with a heart full of anticipation and joy, Bracey set forth on this delightful expedition. The adventure was just beginning, and he couldn't wait to share the wonders of the United Kingdom with fellow young explorers like him.

Join Bracey Beeks on this fascinating journey as he unveils the magic of British culture, a journey that celebrates diversity, fosters friendship, and encourages understanding among the young hearts of the world.

Chapter 2: Discovering Cultures

Bracey, the young explorer, believed that to truly understand the beauty of the UK's culture, he needed to dive into the fascinating world of cultures itself. Exploring the Richness of World Cultures

With his adventurous spirit, Bracey delved into learning about various cultures worldwide. He learned that culture was like a kaleidoscope, each twist revealing a new pattern, a unique story.

He explored the diversity of cultures within the United Kingdom itself - the vibrant Scottish traditions, the rich Welsh heritage, the unique blend of Irish culture, and the intriguing mix of English traditions. Each had its distinct customs, festivals, and ways of life.

Beyond the UK, he discovered the tapestry of cultures from around the world - the vibrant celebrations in India, the ancient traditions of China, the diverse practices of Africa, and the festive spirit of South America. It was a mosaic of humanity, each piece contributing to the beautiful portrait of our global community.

Understanding Our Unique Identities

Bracey realized that culture was not just about the clothes people wore or the food they ate. It was a blend of history, traditions, values, and the people themselves. Every culture had its unique story, shaped by generations and generations of individuals.

He began to understand that each person had a unique identity, influenced by their cultural background, experiences, and upbringing. Just as the UK had its unique cultural identity, so did every individual within it.

With this newfound knowledge, Bracey was ready to dive deeper into the UK's culture, to unravel the stories that made it unique, and to celebrate the richness of humanity that existed within its borders.

The journey into the heart of British culture had just begun, and Bracey was eager to embrace every aspect of it. There was so much to learn, so much to celebrate, and so much magic waiting to be discovered in the United Kingdom.

British Kids

Chapter 3: Clothing Around the Globe

Kids' Fashion: A Kaleidoscope of Styles

Bracey was fascinated by how clothing could speak a silent language about a person's culture, style, and identity.

He believed that understanding what children wore in the UK would give him a glimpse into the heart of British culture.

He set out to explore the stylish and diverse clothing worn by children in the UK. The fashion was like a kaleidoscope of colors, patterns, and designs, each telling a unique story.

In urban areas, Bracey noticed children donning modern, trendy attire. T-shirts with playful prints, jeans of various shades, and sneakers in vibrant colors were popular choices. It was a reflection of the dynamic and fast-paced lifestyle of the cities.

As he traveled to more rural parts of the UK, he observed a shift in clothing styles. Children wore clothing that seemed more connected to nature, often donning earthy tones and comfortable, practical attire suitable for outdoor adventures.

During his exploration, Bracey realized that clothing was not just about looking good; it was a way for children to express themselves and their cultural heritage. In the UK, traditional outfits were often seen during special occasions and events, celebrating the rich history and diversity of the nation.

He saw children wearing kilts in Scotland, honoring their Scottish roots. Welsh children proudly displayed the distinctive patterns and designs on their traditional Welsh dresses.

Understanding the significance of clothing in British culture, Bracey felt a deeper connection with the people and their way of life. He realized that clothing was more than just fabric; it was a representation of culture, history, and personal expression.

With this newfound understanding, Bracey was

eager to explore more aspects of British culture. The adventure into the fascinating world of the UK was unfolding, and the cultural tapestry was just beginning to reveal its vibrant and diverse threads.

Chapter 4: Delicious Adventures: Kids and Food

Tasting the World: Kids and Cuisine

Bracey knew that one of the best ways to unravel the heart of British culture was through its food. Food was not just about taste; it was a window into the culture and history of a place.

In the United Kingdom, he found a delightful array of dishes. The aroma of a classic

English breakfast greeted him each morning - eggs, bacon, sausages, beans, and toast. It was a hearty and comforting start to the day, reflecting the culture's love for a wholesome meal.

He explored the world of pies, from the iconic beef and ale pie to the comforting shepherd's pie. Pies were a quintessential part of British cuisine, loved by both young and old.

Fish and chips were a favorite among children. Bracey discovered that it was a tradition dating back centuries, symbolizing the UK's connection to the sea.

In Wales, he tasted Welsh cakes, a sweet treat that left a delightful taste in his mouth. He realized that every region had its own special delicacies, adding to the richness of British cuisine.

Bracey also had the opportunity to try a variety of teas, learning about the UK's love for a good cuppa. The British tea culture was about more than just the beverage; it was about taking a break, relaxing, and enjoying the moment.

Through these delicious adventures, Bracey understood that food was a way of bringing people together. It was a celebration of culture, a connection to the past, and a taste of the present.

He realized that just like the different flavors that came together to create a delicious dish, cultures too were a blend of various elements - history, traditions, languages, and people.

With each bite, Bracey felt closer to the heart of British culture. He understood that every culture had its unique flavors, and by savoring them, one could truly appreciate the magic of that culture.

As the aroma of delicious British food surrounded him, Bracey was excited for more culinary adventures that lay ahead. The journey into the wonders of the UK's culture had only just begun, and the flavors of Britain were beckoning him further into the heart of this beautiful land.

A Peek into the Lives of Children Worldwide

Bracey was eager to immerse himself in the daily lives of children in the UK, as he believed that understanding their routines and activities would give him a deeper insight into British culture.

He woke up early one morning and joined a group of children in a quaint village. Their day began with getting ready for school - a routine that was followed by children across the UK.

At school, he noticed how enthusiastic and engaged the children were in their studies. They participated in various activities, learned about history, science, literature, and more. Education was a crucial part of their lives, laying the foundation for their future.

During breaks, children would often play games like football (soccer), a beloved sport in the UK. It was a time for friendly competition and bonding with friends.

After school, Bracey saw children engaging in creative activities. Some painted, some wrote stories, and others practiced musical instruments. It was a way for them to express themselves and nurture their talents.

In the evening, families gathered for dinner. It was a time for them to share stories about their day, laugh together, and enjoy a delicious meal. Family was at the heart of their daily lives. As he spent more time with the children, Bracey realized that their routines were not vastly different from those of children in other parts of the world. The essence of childhood remained the same - learning, playing, creating, and spending time with loved ones.

He understood that these routines were like threads weaving the fabric of British society, instilling values, knowledge, and happiness in the young hearts.

With a sense of fulfillment, Bracey continued his journey, excited to explore more aspects of British culture. The glimpse into a day in a kid's life had given him a valuable perspective, allowing him to appreciate the beauty of simplicity and the joys of childhood across the globe.

Chapter 6: Respect and Tradition

Honoring Elders: A Cultural Perspective

Bracey was aware that every culture had its own way of showing respect to elders, a value deeply ingrained in the fabric of society. He was eager to learn how British children demonstrated respect towards their elders, knowing it was a cornerstone of their culture.

He began by observing family gatherings and social interactions. In the UK, children showed respect to elders through simple gestures such as saying "please" and "thank you." These expressions of politeness were essential in their daily communication. During family gatherings, Bracey noticed children listening attentively when elders spoke. It was a way of acknowledging their wisdom and experience. The younger generation valued the knowledge passed down by their elders and often sought their guidance.

In schools, students showed respect to their teachers by following classroom rules, paying attention in class, and addressing them with appropriate titles like "Mr." or "Miss." It was a mark of respect for their educators and the knowledge they shared. Traditions also played a significant role in showing respect. Bracey learned that during certain events or celebrations, children would participate in traditions like bowing or curtsying to elders. These actions were a symbol of honor and respect for their older family members.

He understood that these practices were not just about manners; they were a way of fostering a sense of community and unity. By showing respect to elders, children were preserving the values and traditions passed down through generations.

Bracey was impressed by the genuine respect and care British children demonstrated towards their elders. It was a reminder that no matter where in the world, honoring and respecting those who came before us was a universal value, one that connected us all.

With a newfound understanding of this cultural perspective, Bracey felt a deeper connection to the people and traditions of the UK. The journey into the heart of British culture was unfolding beautifully, and he was excited to continue unraveling the magic that lay within this captivating land.

Chapter 7: Language and Communication

Speaking the World's Languages

Bracey was excited to explore the diverse linguistic landscape of the United Kingdom, understanding that language was an essential part of any culture. He knew that learning a few basic words in British English would help him connect with the local children and better understand the culture.

He began by learning common greetings like "hello," "good morning," and "thank you." These simple words held immense power as they built bridges of communication and showed respect to the people he interacted with.

As he interacted with British children, Bracey realized how language was a key to understanding their culture and forming meaningful connections. The nuances of British English, the different accents and expressions, added a unique flavor to their conversations.

In addition to English, he learned about the preservation of languages like Welsh and Gaelic in certain regions of the UK. It was fascinating to see how diversity in languages was celebrated, and how they were an integral part of the cultural mosaic.

Bracey also discovered the joy of linguistic diversity, understanding that each language was like a window into a culture's soul. It held stories, traditions, and a sense of identity.

He marveled at how people could communicate and understand each other across the world, despite speaking different languages. It was a testament to the power of human connection and the beauty of diversity.

With this newfound appreciation for languages, Bracey felt more connected to the people and culture of the UK. Language was indeed a powerful tool that bridged gaps, allowing us to share our stories, learn from one another, and celebrate the rich tapestry of our global community.

The adventure into the wonders of British culture had given him a deeper understanding of the role language played in fostering connections and preserving traditions. Bracey was eager to continue his journey, embracing the linguistic diversity that made the world a fascinating and beautiful place.

Chapter 8: Friendship Beyond Borders

Making Friends, Bridging Cultures

Friendship, Bracey believed, was the universal language that transcended boundaries and cultures. It was the key to understanding and appreciating the beauty of various cultures.

As Bracey journeyed through the United Kingdom, he

encountered children from diverse backgrounds and regions. Despite their differences, they all shared a common thread - the joy of friendship.

Children in the UK were warm and welcoming, always eager to make new friends. Bracey joined a group of children playing in a park, and to his delight, he was warmly accepted into their games.

Laughter echoed as they played tag, kicking a football, and sharing stories.

Through these interactions, Bracey realized that friendship was a bridge that connected hearts. It didn't matter where you came from or what language you spoke; the language of friendship was universal.

Friendship went beyond borders. It was about

understanding, empathy, and kindness. It was about celebrating differences and finding common ground. It was about sharing a smile, a laugh, and creating beautiful memories together.

He learned that by making friends and building meaningful connections, he was not only enriching his own life but also gaining a deeper understanding of the diverse cultures within the United Kingdom.

With each new friend he made, Bracey felt his horizons expand. He learned about their traditions, their favorite foods, their dreams and aspirations. Friendship was a treasure trove of cultural exchange, and Bracey was eager to collect as many treasures as he could.

As the sun began to set, and it was time to bid his new friends goodbye, Bracey felt a profound sense of gratitude. He understood that the friendships he had made were a glimpse into the beauty of the UK's culture, a culture that valued warmth, openness, and the bonds that tied people together.

The adventure into the heart of British culture was filled with the laughter and camaraderie of newfound friends. Bracey was excited to continue this journey, to make more friends, and to explore the depths of friendship beyond borders. For he knew that in the world of friendship, every heart was a friend waiting to be discovered.

Chapter 9: Greetings Across Continents

Hello, Bonjour, Namaste: How Kids Greet Each Other

Bracey's journey through the United Kingdom had been a delightful adventure filled with discoveries about British culture. He had learned about clothing, food, daily life, respect, language, friendship, and more. But there was one aspect he found particularly fascinating – how children greeted each other in the UK and around the world.

In the UK, he discovered that a friendly "hello" was the most common way for children to greet each other. It was a simple yet warm gesture that opened the door to friendship.

But the world was a vast and diverse place, and Bracey wanted to know how children in other countries greeted each other. He met children from different parts of the world, each teaching him their unique ways of saying hello.

In France, children greeted each other with a cheerful "Bonjour." It was a bright and friendly way to start the day. Bracey tried saying it and felt the warmth it brought to the conversation.

In India, he learned that children often greeted each other with a respectful "Namaste," accompanied by a slight bow. It was a way of showing respect and acknowledging the divine spark within each person. Bracey practiced the gesture and felt a sense of reverence and unity.

As he continued his journey, Bracey encountered even more greetings. In Japan, children bowed politely to each other and said "Konnichiwa." In Spain, a friendly "Hola" filled the air with energy and excitement. In South Africa, children used "Sawubona" to say hello, which meant "I see you," acknowledging each other's presence.

Bracey realized that these greetings were like cultural windows, offering a glimpse into the hearts and minds of children from around the world. They reflected the values, traditions, and customs of each culture.

With each greeting he learned, Bracey felt a deeper connection to the people he met. Greetings were not just words; they were bridges that connected hearts, cultures, and continents.

Learning Points:

Exploring British Culture: Fashion, Cuisine, and Lifestyle

Learning Greetings and Language in the UK

Activity:

Bracey invites young readers to learn a few basic words in British English and use them in a short story, incorporating elements of British culture and greetings.

This activity encourages children to embrace linguistic diversity and celebrate the richness of different cultures.

Kids Across Kulture Book 2
"Bracey Beeks Discovers the UK Wonders"

By
Peter Clarke

Kids
Across
Kulture

Chinese
Kids

American Kids

British Kids

Indian Kids

Canada
Kids

Russian
Kids

alian Kids

French
Kids

Nigeria
Kids

South-
Africa Kids

Egypt Kids

Ghana Kids

Turkey Kids

Kenya Kids

Made in the USA
Columbia, SC
07 November 2023

25627692R00046